SIX **QUESTIONS** OF AMERICAN HISTORY

WHAT DIFFERENCE COULD A WATERWAY MAKE?

And Other Questions about the Erie Canal

Susan Bivin Aller

LERNER PUBLICATIONS COMPANY · MINNEAPOLIS

A Word about Language

English word usage, spelling, grammar, and punctuation have changed over the centuries. We have preserved original spellings and word usage in the quotations included in this book.

Lerner Publications Company
A division of Lerner Publishing Group, Inc.
241 First Avenue North
Minneapolis, MN 55401 U.S.A.

Website address: www.lernerbooks.com

Library of Congress Cataloging-in-Publication Data

Aller, Susan Bivin.
    What Difference Could a Waterway Make? And Other Questions about the
Erie Canal / by Susan Bivin Aller.
        p. cm. — (Six questions of American history)
    Includes bibliographical references and index.
    ISBN 978–1–58013–667–9 (lib. bdg. : alk. paper)
    1. Erie Canal (N.Y.)—History—Juvenile literature. I. Title.
HE396.E6A68 2011
386'.4809747—dc22   2009035565

Manufactured in the United States of America
1 – DP – 7/15/10

TABLE OF CONTENTS

THE SIX QUESTIONS HELP YOU DISCOVER THE FACTS!

INTRODUCTION

On a sparkling November day in 1825, Governor De Witt Clinton of New York stood on the deck of a steamship in New York City's harbor. Thousands of people cheered as he slowly poured water from Lake Erie into the Atlantic Ocean. This "Wedding of the Waters" marked the end of one of the biggest engineering projects of the nineteenth century. A new canal connected Lake Erie to the Atlantic Ocean.

The governor—and the barrel of water—had taken nine days to sail from Buffalo, New York, to the Atlantic Ocean. Horses towed his canal boat 363 miles (584 kilometers) through the new canal to Albany, New York. There, the boat entered the Hudson River. Then steamships pulled it 150 miles (241 km) down the Hudson River to New York City. Crowds along the way cheered the governor and the long line of boats that trailed behind. As the joyful water parade sailed past, bands played and fireworks lit up the sky. At every stop, the governor and his fellow passengers heard speeches and attended parties. New York State had good reason to celebrate. Why was this canal so important? After all, it was just a 40-foot-wide (12-meter) ditch, filled with 4 feet (1 m) of water.

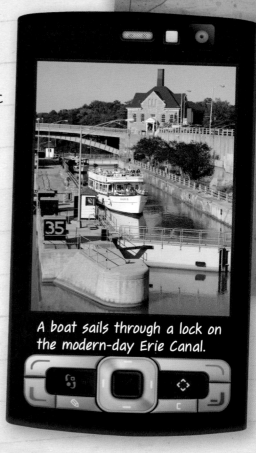

A boat sails through a lock on the modern-day Erie Canal.

BUFFALO

LAKE ERIE

The governor of New York, De Witt Clinton, pours water from Lake Erie into New York Harbor in 1825. This mural of the event was painted in 1905.

ONE FINISHING NATURE'S WORK

The original thirteen colonies of the United States lay along the eastern edge of North America, near the Atlantic Ocean. The Appalachian Mountains were to the west of these colonies. The Appalachians ran from Canada to Georgia. They formed a wall 1,000 miles (1,609 km) long. There were only a few natural breaks, or gaps, where people could get through to the west.

To go westward, people had to travel over rough trails through the gaps. They could also take the long way around by sea. Trading back and forth was almost impossible. The cost to send goods 30 miles (48 km) over

the mountains was the same as sending them across the ocean to Europe. What America needed was a way to carry goods and people through the mountains.

The American Revolution (1775–1783) ended Britain's rule over the United States. This land included the original thirteen colonies. The area also included what Americans called the frontier. These lands would become the modern-day states of Ohio, Indiana, Michigan, Wisconsin, Illinois, and part of Minnesota. The Mississippi River flowed through some of these areas.

People wanted to explore the frontier. Many planned to settle there and build new lives. Travel was so difficult that they might never return. They might even form a separate country.

the war in which the American colonies won their independence from Great Britain

They might even become loyal to France, Spain, or British Canada. Those powerful countries controlled most of the North American continent west of the Mississippi River.

Could the United States somehow tie the western frontier to the eastern states? The country would need to build a canal through the mountains to do so. A canal would link rivers and ports in the East with lakes and rivers in the West. To become a great nation, Americans believed that they needed to finish the work nature had begun. They needed to build a water highway where nature had failed to put one.

Benjamin Franklin, a great American statesman, scientist, and inventor, liked the idea of canals. So did George

WATERY NETWORK

By the early 1800s, many canals operated in the world. Some were as old as recorded history. The Babylonians built the first ones about four thousand years ago. The term *canal* comes from the Latin word *canalis*, meaning "pipe" or "channel." Canals linked rivers, lakes, and seas to one another in a watery network free of tides and currents.

A relief carving from the 800s B.C. shows a city in Iraq surrounded by a network of canals.

Washington, the Revolutionary War general and first U.S. president. The advantages of canals were clear. Canals were quiet and very manageable. Flat-bottomed boats floated along on calm water. They were pulled by ropes harnessed to horses or mules. The animals walked beside the canal on towpaths. Man-made canals could join lakes and rivers to one another in a giant version of connect the dots.

paths for animals towing boats

People suggested various routes through the Appalachians. One of the first people to suggest a canal through New York was the well-known politician Gouverneur Morris. As early as 1777, he predicted that "at no very distant day, the waters of the great inland seas (the Great Lakes) would, by the aid of man, break through their barriers and mingle with those of the Hudson."

"At no very distant day, the waters of the [Great Lakes] would, by the aid of man, break through their barriers and mingle with those of the Hudson."

Gouverneur Morris

Thirty years later, in 1807, a merchant named Jesse Hawley wrote articles describing a likely route. The New York surveyor general, James Geddes, went to explore the route. New Yorkers then gave the survey to President Thomas Jefferson. They asked the U.S. government to pay for a canal. They pointed out that the whole country, not just New York State, would profit from it.

But more important problems were on Jefferson's mind. He had closed all seaports to trading because of British attacks on U.S. ships. Business had dropped off at U.S. port cities. The United States couldn't possibly spare money for a canal. "Why, sir," Jefferson said, "you talk of making a canal 350 miles (560 km) long through the wilderness. It is little short of madness to think of it at this day."

New Yorkers didn't take no for an answer. If the U.S. government wouldn't help them build a canal, they would do it themselves.

"Why, sir, you talk of making a canal 350 miles (560 km) long through the wilderness. It is little short of madness to think of it at this day."

Thomas Jefferson

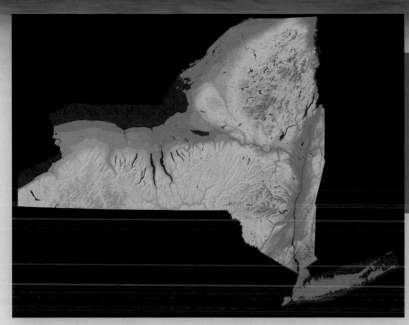

This satellite image shows a relief map of New York State. The high areas are brown, while the dark green areas show river valleys and lowlands.

In 1810 the New York legislature named a group of men to explore the western part of the state. Their job was to suggest how and where to build a waterway to Lake Erie.

a group of elected people with the power to make or change laws

Gouverneur Morris served as senior member of this group. After thirty-three years, he was still excited about a canal. The other men were rich New York landowners and politicians.

NEXT QUESTION

WHO IS MOST CLOSELY LINKED TO THE ERIE CANAL PROJECT?

TWO ROUGH SAILING

The person who played the most important role in the canal project was De Witt Clinton. Clinton would enjoy a long political career. In 1810 he was serving one of his many terms as mayor of New York City. (Later, he would also serve as governor of New York.) Clinton had the political power and the energy to make the project succeed.

On July 4, 1810, Morris, Clinton, and other explorers

De Witt Clinton

headed west from Schenectady, New York. They planned to find a way for a canal to go across New York to Lake Erie. De Witt Clinton kept a journal of the fifty-three-day trip. His words give a colorful account of travel in the early 1800s. The men saw wild and unspoiled landscapes, such as Niagara Falls. They stayed in inns or camped out. At one inn, they were bothered by mosquitoes whizzing around their heads and by bats, crickets, and rats. When they got out of bed, they were covered with bedbugs and fleas.

The exploration party ended its trip near the grand Niagara Falls. This painting was done in 1835, after the canal opened but before millions of tourists visited the natural wonder each year.

When they returned home, the group reported back to the lawmakers. They said a waterway should be built and controlled by New York State. Lawmakers agreed. They asked the group to buy land and get loans to build the canal.

Some New Yorkers didn't want such a huge public works project. They said a canal was going to cost too much money. It would change the landscape. Canal boats would bring crime and disease to towns along the way. People who wanted the canal said new towns and businesses would grow along its route. Shippers would pay tolls on goods that traveled down the canal. That would bring money to local banks and businesses.

public works project: a project—such as a canal, road, or bridge—that all people can use

tolls: money paid to travel on canals, roads, bridges, or other public works

Planning came to a sudden stop in June 1812, when the United States declared war on Great Britain. Britain had caused more trouble to shipping and trading on the Atlantic Ocean. Fighting began in what became the War of 1812 (1812–1815). Some of the bloodiest battles

CLINTON'S DITCH

De Witt Clinton's name is always associated with the Erie Canal. In fact, critics often called it Clinton's Ditch, or Clinton's Folly. During the War of 1812, Clinton ran for president of the United States. He was a peace candidate. He lost, and James Madison was reelected president. Both Clinton and Madison were Republicans. Clinton's campaign divided the Republican Party. Clinton's political enemies wanted to get even. So they voted against his canal project when he was governor of New York. They also voted him off the Canal Commission. But De Witt Clinton believed in the canal and fought hard to make it happen.

In a heroic move in a battle on Lake Erie during the War of 1812, U.S. admiral Oliver Hazard Perry (standing) sailed toward a British ship to take control of it and to win the battle.

took place in New York on and around Lake Erie and Lake Ontario. The United States fought hard to keep control of Lake Erie. The luke was a critical link to the western frontier.

When the war ended three years later, Lake Erie was safe in U.S. hands. New Yorkers knew the way to the American West was through Lake Erie. Some people had wanted a canal to lead to Lake Ontario. But Lake Ontario's main outlet for shipping was through the Saint Lawrence River to Canadian ports rather than U.S. ports. The planners drew the route from Albany to Lake Erie. The canal would pass through or near the towns of Schenectady, Utica, Syracuse, Rochester, and Buffalo.

A woodcut print shows the first settlement in Rochester, New York, in 1812. The population numbered just fifteen people the year before.

The planners of the canal needed support from the public. They organized meetings all over New York State. At those meetings, planners read a letter from De Witt Clinton. His powerful arguments in favor of a canal reached thousands of people. After listening to Clinton's words, more than one hundred thousand people sent letters to the New York legislature supporting the canal.

A canal bill passed the legislature in 1816. The legislature decided to build the canal in three sections. There would be a western, a middle, and an eastern section. Construction would begin with the middle section, called the Long Level.

WHAT WAS THE LONG LEVEL?

The Long Level was the section of the Erie Canal that ran between Seneca Falls and Utica.

This section ran about 90 miles (145 km) between Seneca Falls and Utica. The land there was almost flat. It was a good place for new designers and workers to start. But with construction about to begin, people asked, "Where are the workers?"

NEXT QUESTION

WHERE WOULD ENOUGH CANAL WORKERS BE FOUND?

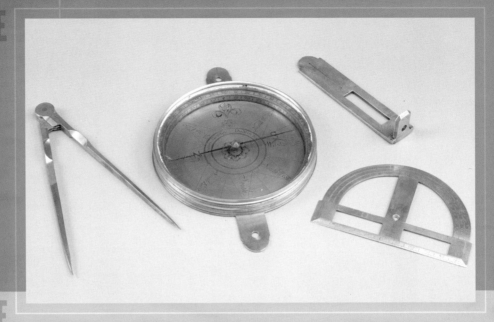

Surveyors used tools like these to map areas of land. They measured distances and land features to decide where the canal should run.

THREE CHANGING THE FACE OF THE EARTH

Building the canal would be hard. The most difficult part of the job was finding men who knew how to design and build canals. There were no civil engineers in the United States. The nearest thing to an engineer was a surveyor.

The planners hired the best surveyors they knew. These included James Geddes, Benjamin Wright, Charles Broadhead, and later Canvass White and Nathan Roberts. Benjamin Wright became chief engineer for the first section. The surveyors and their staff solved the huge challenges that faced them. The Erie Canal became a training ground for civil engineers in the United States.

On July 1, 1817, De Witt Clinton became governor of New York. As governor he was in a strong position to lead the canal project to completion. Three days later, on the Fourth of July, a large crowd gathered in Rome, New York. Americans celebrated their country's history and their hopes for the future.

As the sun rose, cannons boomed. Judge John Richardson drove his team of oxen forward. They pulled a plow that broke ground for the Erie Canal. He had the honor of making the first cut because he had signed the first construction contract. Most men had brought shovels to the ceremony. As the cannon boomed again, they plunged them into the soft earth. Everybody was eager to take part in this great historic event.

contract an agreement supported by law

The planners gave out about fifty contracts for work on the first section. The men who got contracts were farmers, carpenters, mechanics, or businessmen.

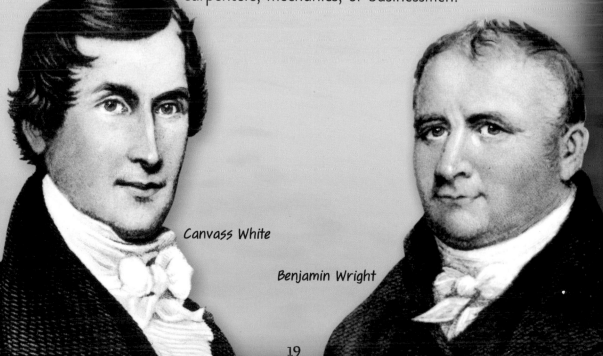

Canvass White

Benjamin Wright

Local workers helped build sections of the canal in their own homelands. John William Hill painted this scene near Little Falls, New York, in 1831.

Most of them owned land in the canal's path. They brought many skills to their work. They wanted to be proud of the sections they built through their own lands. Each hired his own laborers and brought his own tools. Most of the laborers were local men. They knew how to cut down trees and dig out the stumps to make way for the canal bed.

First, surveyors put in two rows of red wooden stakes. The stakes were set 60 feet (18 m) apart. They marked the path where Richardson and his men began to clear the land. Between these rows, the surveyors had set two more rows of stakes, 40 feet (12 m) apart. That marked where the ditch would be dug. The finished canal would be 40 feet wide at the top of the channel. It tapered in a U-shape to 28 feet (9 m) wide at the bottom. Water in the canal would be 4 feet (1 m) deep. A towpath would run along one side for the horses and mules that towed the boats. A berm, or ridge of earth, would be built on the other side for people to walk or ride on.

The canal was not a natural waterway. That meant it needed to be filled with water from other sources. Workers dug channels to lakes or streams that were higher than the canal. Water flowed downhill from them into the canal. Canal workers controlled the flow by opening and closing sluices.

gates that control the flow of water

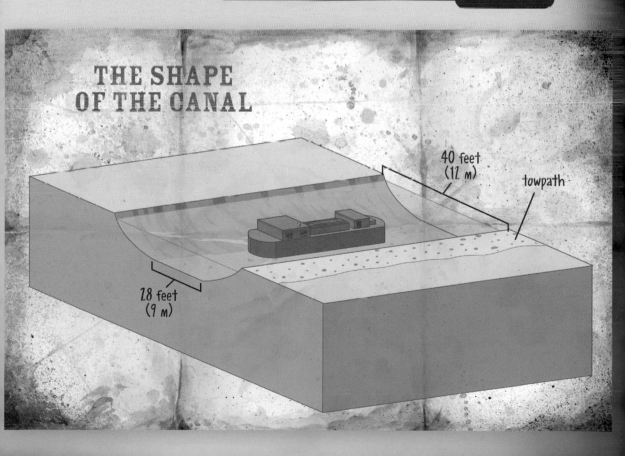

THE SHAPE OF THE CANAL

40 feet (12 m)

towpath

28 feet (9 m)

WORKERS ON THE ERIE CANAL

On July 4, 1817, six months after the groundbreaking ceremony, a thousand men were at work building the canal. Most of the men who worked on the first sections of the canal came from nearby towns and farms. Some were freed slaves. Then crops failed in Ireland, a country in Europe. To keep from starving, thousands of Irish moved from Ireland to New York. By 1822 as many as three thousand Irishmen were at work on the famous locks at Lockport, near the western end of the canal.

When a contractor finished his part of the canal, he could apply for a contract to do another section. Each section could be filled with water or drained without involving the sections on either end.

The designers and workers didn't have an easy job. In the early 1800s, western New York State was covered with thick forests.

Forested lands and steep hillsides through the planned canal area made things difficult for builders.

Workers had to make the canal pass through or around steep-sided hills. Towpaths were built along the sides of the canal.

Many trees had to be cut down. Except for the Long Level, the land was not flat. The canal had to go through, over, or around cliffs, valleys, wide rivers, waterfalls, and rock formations. Workers had no power machinery of any sort. They also faced dangers from wild animals, disease, and extreme weather.

NEXT QUESTION

HOW COULD CANAL WORKERS OVERCOME ALL THESE NATURAL BARRIERS?

WHO
WHAT
WHERE
WHY
WHEN
HOW
WHO
WHAT
WHERE
WHY
WHEN
HOW
WHO
WHAT
WHY
WHEN

Workers on the Erie Canal did not have heavy machinery to cut through rock. They removed the large amounts of dirt and soil by hand.

FOUR SOLVING PROBLEMS

Americans had never taken on such a large public works project. The men in charge solved problems and learned as they went along. No other canals of that size were around to use as models. Workers sweated over their shovels until they made a level, watertight channel. They got eight to twelve dollars a month. That was good pay in those days. But the labor was tiring and often dangerous. Explosives blasting through rock sent flying debris that killed or injured some men. Collapses of the canal bed and quicksand buried others. In the summer of 1819, workers were in mosquito-infested areas near the

rock fragments; the remains of something destroyed

Seneca River. More than a thousand men became ill or died of malaria, a serious disease carried by mosquitoes. When the ground froze in winter, digging stopped and the men were laid off.

The common sense of these men explains much of the canal's success. When workers didn't have the tools or materials they needed, they invented something. For example, they designed a huge horse-drawn machine to help them cut through the forests. It could uproot thirty to forty tree stumps in a day. That was much more than a crew of men could dig in a day.

Another invention solved the problem of cementing limestone blocks in place. The mortar that was ordinarily used to hold the blocks together became soft under water. One of the surveyors, Canvass White, began experimenting.

mortar: a building material that hardens to hold pieces together

This modern photo shows how blocks of rock were cemented together to form the walls in the Erie Canal.

He discovered that a certain local limestone could be made into hydraulic cement. White's cement soon became the best waterproof cement in the country.

Engineers faced a big problem trying to make the canal perfectly level. Boats couldn't go uphill or downhill. But Lake Erie, at the western end of the canal, was 565 feet (172 m) higher than the Hudson River on the eastern end. Some people suggested that the canal be built on a slightly tilted plane. That way it would be a level, gently sloping line from one end to the other. But the route of the canal couldn't be made that way. It dipped into deep valleys and river gorges. At other spots, it climbed over hills and rocky cliffs.

The engineers solved the problem by building locks. Locks are waterproof boxes big enough to hold canal boats. They

BOATS CLIMBING STEPS

Leonardo da Vinci was a famous Italian artist. He studied the movement of water. In the 1400s, he designed the first canal locks. The locks on the Erie Canal work the same as his did.

The Erie Canal's locks are watertight boxes that are 8 feet (2 m) deep. That's big enough to hold a canal boat. At each end, a pair of V-shaped gates point upstream. The pressure of water trying to flow downstream pushes against the gates. That keeps them closed. When a boat wants to go upstream, it waits for the gates to open. Then it enters the lock. The gates behind it close. The gates at the upstream end open to let in water. As water fills the lock, the boat floats up to the level of the next lock. Then the front gates open. The boat moves into the second lock and so on. When a boat is going downstream, the process is reversed.

are lined with limestone blocks. The blocks are held in place by Canvass White's cement. They work like giant steps. Locks let boats "climb" up or down between different levels on the canal. As workers close or open gates, the locks fill with or empty water. Boats in the locks float up or down. When the boats reach the level of the next section of the canal, the lock gates open and the boats move on.

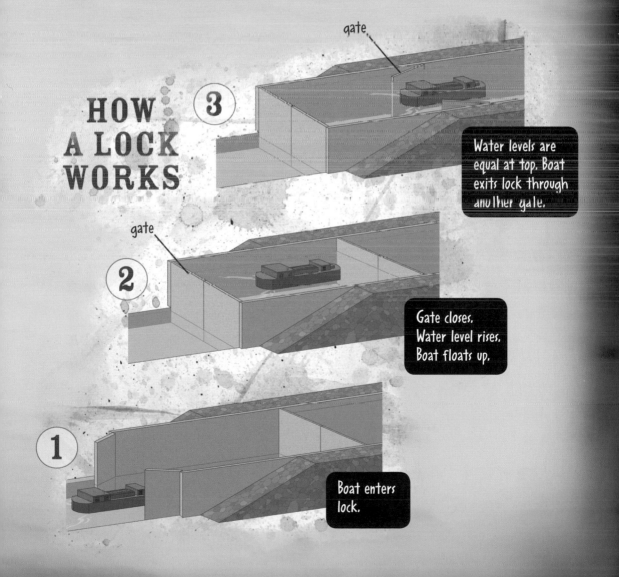

gate

HOW A LOCK WORKS

3 — Water levels are equal at top. Boat exits lock through another gate.

gate

2 — Gate closes. Water level rises. Boat floats up.

1 — Boat enters lock.

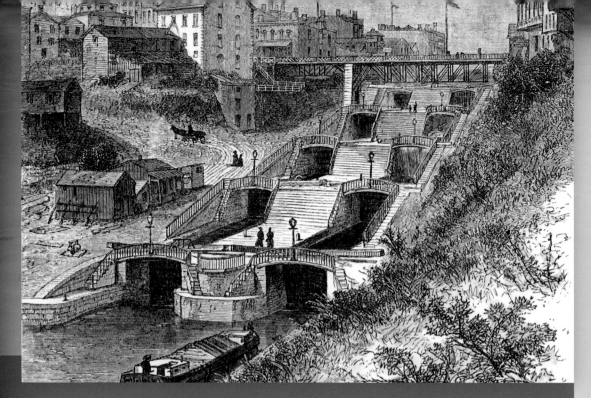

A series of five locks helped boats up the steep section of the canal at Lockport.

The most amazing locks were built at Lockport. Nathan Roberts designed a set of five locks. They looked like two staircases side by side. Boats heading one direction went up one flight. At the same time, boats going the other direction went down the other flight. That prevented traffic jams. But even these great locks couldn't climb high enough for boats to get over the rock cliff at Lockport. Workers spent three years blasting through 7 miles (11 km) of solid rock. This section is called the Deep Cut. At some places, the rock walls on either side of the canal rise 30 feet (9 m) above the canal bed.

In addition to eighty-three locks, workers built more than three hundred bridges. They connected fields and roads that had been separated by the canal. Some of the bridges were so low that they barely cleared the tops of boats passing beneath. In songs of the Erie Canal, one of the most popular lines is "low bridge, everybody down!" At that shout, people sitting on top of a boat would fling themselves flat or suffer being knocked down.

Engineers also built eighteen aqueducts. Aqueducts carry boats across gorges and rivers. They were built of stone and looked like bridges. Some aqueducts carried water for drinking or irrigating crops. But the Erie Canal aqueducts carried water for boats to float on.

large channels that bring water from far away

Of all the aqueducts on the Erie Canal, workers built the largest one over the Genesee River at Rochester. It was three city blocks long (about 800 feet, or 244 meters) and held 2,000 tons (1,800 metric tons) of water. The aqueduct took two years and the labor of hundreds of workers to complete. Most of the workers were Irish immigrants. In October 1823, it opened with a parade of decorated boats sailing overhead. Bands played and people cheered. Excitement grew as the canal neared completion.

people who move from one country to live in another

NEXT QUESTION

WHAT CHANGES DID THE ERIE CANAL BRING TO THE TOWNS AND CITIES ALONG ITS ROUTE?

WHO
WHAT
WHERE
WHY
WHEN
HOW
WHO
WHAT
WHERE
WHY
WHEN
WHO
WHAT
WHERE
WHY
WHEN

These barges have crossed the aqueduct *(left)* that was built to go over the Genesee River in Rochester.

FIVE WEDDING OF THE WATERS

Workers connected the sections of the canal to one another as the sections were finished. By 1822 the canal was open to barge traffic for 180 miles (290 km). People felt the changes almost at once. Towns and businesses grew quickly along the canal. Boats that traveled on the canal paid a toll. How much money a boat paid was based on weight and distance traveled. People had predicted that traffic would reach 250,000 tons (227,000 metric tons) in twenty years. It reached 750,000 tons (680,000 metric tons) in half that time.

The total cost was about seven million dollars (four billion

a large boat with a flat bottom

in modern-day dollars). But profits soon flowed in. The canal rapidly began to pay for itself. It was clearly a huge success. During the first year the canal was finished, thirteen thousand boats and forty thousand people traveled on it.

On October 26, 1825, Governor De Witt Clinton led a parade from the Buffalo courthouse to the waterfront at Lake Erie. He stepped onto a gaily decorated passenger boat named the *Seneca Chief.* Jesse Hawley, whose original plan for the canal had started the ball rolling in 1807, gave a speech. New York, he said, had "made the longest canal, in the least time, with the least experience, for the least money, and of the greatest public utility of any other in the world."

Governor De Witt Clinton and a group of statesmen and their wives travel on the *Seneca Chief* toward New York Harbor. This mural was painted by C. Y. Turner in 1905 for a high school named after Clinton.

Utica, New York, pictured in 1850. The Erie Canal turned many villages, such as Utica, along its route into bustling cities.

THE NEW YORK MIRACLE

Supporters had said that the Erie Canal would quickly pay for itself. They thought great economic growth would follow its path. And they were right. At Lockport, for example, the population grew from 3 families to 337 when lock digging began. Two and a half years later, Lockport had a population of three thousand people. Almost two thousand Irish laborers also stayed on after building the locks. New York City felt the most impact of all. It had always been a major port city. Then the Erie Canal linked it to the American West. New York City became the most important center of trade, transportation, and finance in the United States.

At 10:00 A.M. the *Seneca Chief* moved into the waters of the canal. Cannons were lined up at points all the way to New York City. They were placed within earshot of one another. One after the other, they boomed. At last the firing, or cannonade, reached Sandy Hook, New Jersey, in New York's harbor. Then the firing

cannonade, a heavy fire of artillery

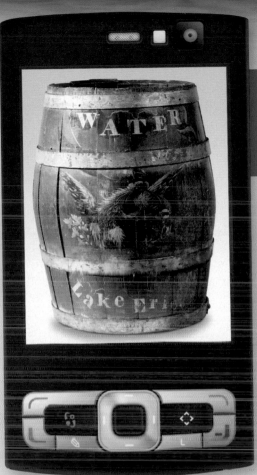

This is one of the two barrels that held water from Lake Erie as it made the trip along the canal to the Atlantic Ocean.

began again from the harbor back to Buffalo. The round-trip cannon fire took more than two hours to complete. Clinton's parade was on its way.

The *Seneca Chief*'s most important cargo was water from Lake Erie. It was contained in two green barrels with golden bands. One of the boats in the parade was named *Noah's Ark*. It came from the town of Ararat on the Niagara River. The boat carried living symbols of the West, including two Seneca Indian boys, two bears, and two eagles. Another boat, *The Young Lion of the West* from Rochester, held live wolves, raccoons, foxes, and deer from the Rochester area.

For the next week, Clinton and his friends heard fireworks, cannon salutes, and band concerts. They ate feasts given by towns along the canal. They watched balloon flights and theater productions. On November 2, the boats left the canal at Albany and entered the Hudson River.

cargo goods carried by a boat, airplane, or other vehicle

The next morning, eight steamships pulled the canal boats down the Hudson toward New York City, 150 miles (241 km) away. Welcoming ships sailed with them. On the bright morning of November 4, more than forty ships steamed into New York's harbor and down to Sandy Hook. That is where New York's harbor meets the Atlantic Ocean. In the ocean, the canal boats seemed very small. But their trip gave them a large place in U.S. history.

WHERE IS NEW YORK HARBOR?
New York Harbor is where the Hudson River flows into New York Bay and the Atlantic Ocean.

Ships in New York Harbor welcome the *Seneca Chief* as the ship completed the 150-mile (241 km) journey from Buffalo, New York. Painter Anthony Imbert captured the scene in 1825.

In front of a cheering crowd, Clinton pours water from Lake Erie into the Atlantic Ocean.

De Witt Clinton got off his canal boat and boarded the steamboat *Washington*. It carried the committee of greeters from New York City. After making a short speech, he poured the water from Lake Erie into the Atlantic Ocean. This "Wedding of the Waters" was the high point of the day. After that, everybody formed a long parade and marched to New York's city hall.

After the parties were over, the little canal boat *Seneca Chief* went back up the Hudson River to Albany and then home on the canal to Buffalo. This time it carried a barrel of salty Atlantic seawater to mix with the freshwater of Lake Erie.

NEXT QUESTION

WHEN WOULD TRADE, TRAVEL, AND PEOPLE MAKE USE OF THE CANAL?

A young boy guides horses along the canal's towpath. The horses tow the barge along the canal.

SIX CANALLERS COMING!

As traffic on the canal increased, so did the kinds of people passing through New York. Lockkeepers, toll collectors, and repair workers arrived. Crews for the boats and drivers for the horses and mules on the towpath also came.

These workers were called canallers. They brought money to the state, but they also brought problems. Many of them drank, gambled, and fought. Their language and behavior shocked people who lived along the canal.

Young boys who worked as deckhands or drivers were another problem. Many of them were only eleven or

> **canallers** workers on canal boats and towpaths

twelve years old. Some were orphans or runaways. Their bosses often treated them badly. They grew up into rowdy, uneducated young men. In the long winter months, when the canal froze, these boys had a hard time surviving. Many broke laws and were put in jail. In jail they at least had food and a place to sleep. Social and religious organizations did their best to protect these boys. They also tried to improve living conditions for others who worked on the canal.

Boats with stores and taverns added to the traffic on the canal. A boat called *Encyclopedia* had a bookstore and a museum of natural curiosities. The canal became so crowded that traffic jams occurred. Boats had to wait to go through the locks. Some boats hit one another when captains tried to pass one another on the narrow channel. The speed limit was set at 4 miles (6 km) per hour.

curiosities.
unusual items of general interest

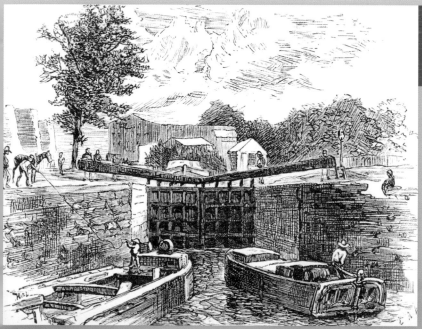

Two boats await entry to a lock in Troy, New York.

A grain boat reaches the Hudson River. Three canallers play music, while a woman brings up more laundry to hang.

Despite these problems, the canal carried the products of farms and factories. From the West came wheat, corn, meat, lumber, and furs. These items were headed to markets in the East and in Europe. From the East came iron, furniture, and other manufactured and imported items heading to towns on the frontier.

The Erie Canal also played an important role in moving people to the West. Only three days after the canal opened in 1825, a boat docked at Buffalo. The boat was carrying fifty emigrants on their way to Michigan.

people who leave one country to live in another

WHERE IS BUFFALO?
Buffalo is on the easternmost end of Lake Erie.

LOW BRDIGE, EVERYBODY DOWN

Here's the first verse and chorus of Thomas Allen's 1905 song about working on the Erie Canal.

I've got an old mule and her name is Sal
Fifteen years on the Erie Canal
She's a good old worker and a good old pal
Fifteen years on the Erie Canal
We've hauled some barges in our day
Filled with lumber, coal, and hay
And every inch of the way we know
From Albany to Buffalo
CHORUS:
Low bridge, everybody down
Low bridge for we're coming to a town
And you'll always know your neighbor
And you'll always know your pal
If you've ever navigated on the Erie Canal

A year later, Buffalo newspapers reported the arrival in a single day of twelve hundred people moving to the West. These people were not all from other countries. Many came from New England states, especially Vermont and New Hampshire.

The Erie Canal also became part of the Underground Railroad. Slaves fleeing their masters in the South used the canal. From Buffalo they had just a short way to go before reaching freedom over the border in Canada.

The Buffalo newspaper described this scene in 1832. "Canal boats filled with emigrants, and covered with goods and furniture, are almost hourly arriving." On Lake Erie, people transferred to steamboats. The steamboats were "literally crammed with masses of living beings," the paper continued, "... their decks piled up in huge heaps with furniture and [belongings] of all descriptions." One observer said it looked as if all Europe was moving to America!

The Erie Canal earned back the cost of its construction through tolls in only nine years. New York City became the busiest U.S. port. This happened mainly because of its connection to the canal. Almost every major city in New York State is near the canal's path. Even in modern times, 80 percent of upstate New York's population lives within 25 miles (40 km) of the Erie Canal.

The Erie Canal did more than open a waterway for trade and travel through the Appalachians. It opened world markets to the United States. The canal gave the country a chance to become an international leader of business and industry.

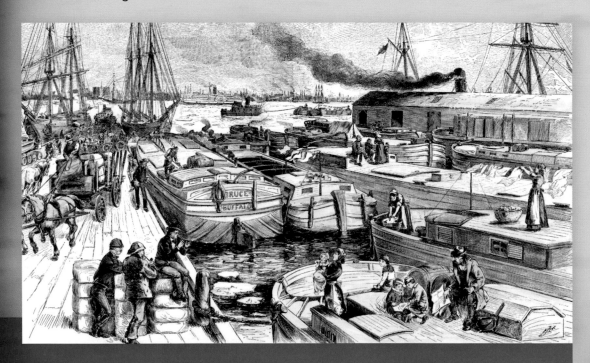

Docks in New York City are full of trade goods brought down the Erie Canal on barges.

END OF AN ERA

Engineers enlarged the Erie Canal several times. In 1918 they connected the canal to a statewide network of canals, lakes, and rivers. But by the 1950s, competition from railroads and highways grew. Use of the canal for carrying goods decreased quickly after that.

In the twenty-first century, the Erie Canal is part of the New York State Canal System. The Erie Canalway National Heritage Corridor is a popular tourist and recreation area.

The Erie Canal had a powerful and long-term effect on the development of the United States. If it had not been built, the country and the world would be very different.

The early canal supporters had a vision that inspired the people of New York. Then a group of inexperienced engineers came up with a plan to make that vision a reality. Thousands of men labored eight years to create an engineering miracle. The Erie Canal stands as one of the country's first and most remarkable public works achievements.

NEXT QUESTION

HOW DO WE KNOW SO MUCH ABOUT THE ERIE CANAL?

Primary Source: Tavel Account by Nathaniel Hawthorne

A primary source is something that was written or recorded at the time of an event. Or it can be something that a reliable eyewitness describes soon after the event. This material might be a newspaper article, a letter, or a diary entry. It could be a photograph, a recording, or a painting.

The following is a firsthand account of travel on the Erie Canal in 1835. It was written by the famous U.S. author Nathaniel Hawthorne.

> I embarked [boarded a boat] about thirty miles [48 km] below Utica, determining to voyage along the whole extent of the canal. . . .

> Sometimes we met a black and rusty-looking vessel, laden with lumber, salt from Syracuse, or Genesee flour, and shaped at both ends like a square-toed boot. . . . On its deck would be a square hut, and a woman seen through the window at her household work, with a little tribe of children, who perhaps had been born in this strange dwelling and knew no other home. Thus, while the husband smoked his pipe at the helm, and the eldest son rode one of the horses [on the towpath], on went the family, traveling hundreds of miles in their own house, and carrying their fireside with them. . . .

> Not long after . . . we overtook a vessel that seemed full of mirth and sunshine. It contained a little colony of Swiss, . . . singing, laughing, and making merry. . . . One pretty [girl] . . . addressed a mirthful remark to me; she spoke in her native tongue, and I [replied] in good English, both of us laughing heartily. . . . I cannot describe how pleasantly this incident affected me.

TELL YOUR STORY ABOUT TRAVELING ON THE ERIE CANAL

It is 1830, and you are ten years old. Your family has just moved from a farm south of Albany, New York, to the Territory of Michigan. Part of the way, you traveled on the new Erie Canal. You are writing a letter to your cousin back in New York.

HOW many kinds of transportation did you use to reach Michigan?

WHO else was traveling?

WHERE did you stop along the way?

WHAT did you see and hear along the way?

WHY does your family like living on the frontier?

USE **WHO, WHAT, WHERE WHY, WHEN, AND HOW** TO THINK OF OTHER QUESTIONS TO HELP YOU CREATE YOUR STORY!

Timeline

1775

The thirteen American colonies go to war with Great Britain.

1776

Americans formally declare independence from Great Britain.

1777

New York statesman Gouverneur Morris says a canal could link the Hudson River to the Great Lakes.

1783

The American Revolution ends. The U.S. territory expands to the Mississippi River.

1780s

George Washington promotes the Patowmack Canal in Virginia.

1807

New York merchant Jesse Hawley's essays promote the Erie Canal.

1808

New York sends surveyor James Geddes to explore a planned route.

1809

President Thomas Jefferson turns down New York's request for canal funding.

1810

De Witt Clinton and other canal commissioners survey the area for the canal.

1812

The United States declares war on Great Britain, a move that delays plans for building the Erie Canal.

De Witt Clinton runs for president of the United States.

1816

The New York legislature passes the canal bill, providing funds for the canal.

1817

Construction begins on the Erie Canal at Rome, New York.

De Witt Clinton becomes governor of New York.

Crop failure causes many Irish to emigrate from Ireland to the United States.

1819

The first 98 miles (158 km) of the Erie Canal open.

1823

The aqueduct over the Genesee River is completed.

1825

The canal is completed at a cost of about $7 million.

Governor De Witt Clinton travels from Lake Erie to New York Harbor by boat.

The "Wedding of the Waters" celebrates the opening of the Erie Canal.

Source Notes

9 Gouverneur Morris, quoted in David Hosack, *Memoir of De Witt Clinton,* note O, "Examination of the Claims of Gouveneur Morris Relative to the Erie Canal" (New York: J. Seymour, 1829), 250, available online at http://history.rochester.edu/canal/bib/hosack/APPOO.html (March 30, 2010).

9 Ibid.

10 Thomas Jefferson, quoted in Joshua Forman's letter to David Hosack, in David Hosack, *Memoir of De Witt Clinton* (New York: J. Seymour, 1829), 347, available online at http://history.rochester.edu/canal/bib/hosack/APPOU.html (March 30, 2010).

10 Ibid.

31 Ronald E. Shaw, *Erie Water West: A History of the Erie Canal 1792–1854* (Lexington: University of Kentucky Press, 1966), 184.

39 Ibid., 274.

39 Thomas S. Allen, "Low Bridge, Everybody Down," ErieCanalSong.com, 2009, http://www.eriecanalsong.com/ (April 6, 2010).

42 Nathaniel Hawthorne, "The Canal Boat," *New England Magazine* 9 (December 1835): 398–409, available online at http://www.history.rochester.edu/can/bib/hawthorne/canalboat.htm (March 30, 2010).

Selected Bibliography

Bernstein, Peter L. *Wedding of the Waters: The Erie Canal and the Making of a Great Nation.* New York: W. W. Norton & Co., 2005.

Campbell, William W. *The Life and Writings of De Witt Clinton (Private Canal Journal).* New York: Baker & Scribner, 1849. Available online at University of Rochester. N.d. http://www.history.rochester.edu/canal/bib/campbell/contents.html (December 4, 2009).

Department of History, University of Rochester. "Erie Canal Bibliography." N.d. http://www.history.rochester.edu/canal/bib (December 4, 2009).

Hawthorne, Nathaniel. "The Canal Boat." *New England Magazine* 9 (December 1835): 398–409. Available online at http://www.history.rochester.edu/canal/bib/hawthorne/canalboat.htm (March 29, 2010).

Hosack, David. *Memoir of De Witt Clinton.* New York: J. Seymour, 1829. Available online at http://www.history.rochester.edu/canal/bib/hosack/Memoir.html (March 29, 2010).

Lawson, Dorris Moore. *Nathan Roberts: Erie Canal Engineer.* Edited by Eric W. Lawson Sr. Utica, NY: North Country Books, 1997.

Papp, John. *Erie Canal Days: A Pictorial Essay/Albany to Buffalo.* Schenectady, NY: privately printed, 1967.

Shaw, Ronald E. *Erie Water West: A History of the Erie Canal 1792–1854*. Lexington: University of Kentucky Press, 1966.

Sheriff, Carol. *The Artificial River: The Erie Canal and the Paradox of Progress, 1817–1862*. New York: Hill and Wang, 1996.

Walker, Barbara K., and Warren S. Walker, eds. *The Erie Canal: Gateway to Empire*. Boston: D. C. Heath & Co., 1963.

Further Reading and Websites

Erie Canal Teacher's Guide
http://www.laguardiawagnerarchive.lagcc.cuny.edu/eriecanal/
This site offers a detailed, illustrated explanation of how locks work and weekly records of the cargo shipped to and from New York City and the new frontier.

Gelman, Amy. *New York*. Minneapolis: Lerner Publications Company, 2002. In this book, readers will find information about New York's land, history, economy, and more.

Goldstein, Margaret J. *Irish in America*. Minneapolis: Lerner Publications Company, 2005. Learn about the history of the Irish coming to the United States and how Irish people and culture have become a part of American society.

Harness, Cheryl. *Amazing Impossible Erie Canal*. New York: Aladdin, 1999. A lively text introduces readers to the Erie Canal.

Lourie, Peter. *Erie Canal: Canoeing America's Great Waterway*. Honesdale, PA: Boyds Mills Press, 1999. History and current events weave together in this story of a three-week canoe trip on the Erie Canal.

Myers, Anna. *Hoggee*. New York: Walker & Co., 2004. A boy struggles to survive winter on the Erie Canal.

Social Studies for Kids
http://www.socialstudiesforkids.com/www/us/eriecanaldcf.htm
This site provides a brief history of the Erie Canal and its role in settling the midwestern states. It also provides a detailed map and links to related sites.

Stein, R. Conrad. *The Erie Canal*. New York: Children's Press, 2004. This book presents a simple, illustrated history of the canal.

Index

Photo Acknowledgments

The images in this book are used with the permission of: © iStockphoto.com/DNY59, p. 1; © iStockphoto.com/
Elena Asenova, pp. 1 (background), and all water backgrounds; © iStockphoto.com/sx70, pp. 3 (top), 8
(left), 14, 22 (top), 26, 32 (bottom), 39, 41; © iStockphoto.com/Ayse Nazli Deliormanli, pp. 3 (bottom), 43
(right); © iStockphoto.com/Serdar Yagci, pp. 4–5 (background), 43 (background); © Bill Hauser/Independent
Picture Service, pp. 4–5 (map), 7, 17 (inset), 21, 27, 34 (inset), 38 (inset); © iStockphoto.com/Andrey
Pustovoy, pp. 4, 25, 33; © Andre Jenny/Alamy, p. 4 (inset); DeWitt Clinton High School, New York State
Canal Corporation, pp. 5, 45; © N. Currier/The Bridgeman Art Library/Getty Images, p. 6; © Erich Lessing/
Art Resource, NY, p. 8 (right); © Bristol City Museum and Art Gallery, UK/The Bridgeman Art Library,
p. 9; © Bettmann/CORBIS, p. 10; U.S. Geological Survey/National Elevation Dataset (NED), p. 11; I. N.
Phelps Stokes Collection, Miriam and Ira D. Wallach Division of Art, Prints and Photographs, The New York
Public Library, Astor, Lenox and Tilden Foundations, p. 12 (top); © Collection of the New-York Historical
Society, USA/The Bridgeman Art Library, pp. 12 (bottom), 44; The Granger Collection, New York, pp. 13,
16, 19 (both), 35, 36, 43 (left); Library of Congress, pp. 15 (LC-USZC4-6893), 31 (LC-USZ62-80635);
© iStockphoto.com/Talshiar, pp. 17, 34 (top), 38 (bottom); © Atwater Kent Museum of Philadelphia/Courtesy
of Historical Society of Pennsylvania Collection/The Bridgeman Art Library, p. 18; detail of The Erie Canal
by John William Hill, 1831, watercolor on paper, 16" x 20", courtesy of the Union College Permanent
Collection, Union College, Schenectady, NY, p. 20; © Peter Harholdt/CORBIS, p. 22 (bottom); © SuperStock/
SuperStock, p. 23; © Art Resource, NY, p. 24; AP Photo/Jim McKnight, p. 25 (inset); © North Wind Picture
Archives, pp. 28, 38 (top), 40; Photography Collection, Miriam and Ira D. Wallach Division of Art, Prints and
Photographs, The New York Public Library, Astor, Lenox and Tilden Foundations, p. 30; © The Bridgeman Art
Library/Getty Images, p. 32 (top); Collection of The New-York Historical Society, X.48, p. 33 (inset); The Art
Archive/Museum of the City of New York/49.415.1, p. 34 (bottom); © Antman Archives/The Image Works,
p. 37.

Front cover: The Granger Collection, New York.
Back cover: © iStockphoto.com/Elena Asenova (background).